2001-2 NWMS
MISSION EDUCATION RESOURCES

❊ ❊ ❊

READING BOOKS

BY THE GRACE OF GOD
The Life of Grace Prescott
by Della Hines Newnum

IF MY PEOPLE
The Manny Chavier Story
by Steve Adams

JOURNEYS OF FAITH
From Canada to the World
by Valerie J. Friesen

MISSION IN THE THIRD MILLENNIUM
by Chuck Gailey

MY FATHER'S HOUSE
Nazarene Missions in Samoa
by Francine Duckworth and Nancy Fuga Stephenson

TO THE ENDS OF THE EARTH
Proclaiming the Gospel Through the *JESUS* Film
by L. David Duff

❊ ❊ ❊

ADULT MISSION EDUCATION RESOURCE BOOK

CALLED TO ALL NATIONS
Edited by Wes Eby

If My People

The Manny Chavier Story

by
Steve Adams

Nazarene Publishing House
Kansas City, Missouri

Copyright 2001
by Nazarene Publishing House

ISBN 083-411-8467

Printed in the United States of America

Editor: Wes Eby
Cover Design: Kevin Williamson

10   9   8   7   6   5   4   3   2   1

Contents

"If my people,
which are called by name,
shall humble themselves,
and pray,
and seek my face,
and turn from their wicked ways;
then will I hear from heaven,
and will forgive their sin,
and will heal their land"
(2 Chronicles 7:14, KJV).

Steve Adams, composer and pianist, was born and raised in New England in a Nazarene parsonage. In over 30 years of music ministry, Steve has seen his songs included in hymnals of many evangelical denominations. Tunes such as "Peace in the Midst of the Storm," "All Because of God's Amazing Grace," "Where the Spirit of the Lord Is," and "All in the Name of Jesus" have literally gone around the world. His wife, Janet, their sons, Craig and Chris, and daughter-in-law, Deanna, share in Steve's worldwide music ministry.

Steve possesses a deep interest in inner-city ministries. Having known Rev. and Mrs. Manuel Chavier most of his life, he feels it is a privilege to chronicle their story and their ministry in International Church of the Nazarene in New Bedford, Massachusetts. "The greatest song anyone can write," he insists, "is one of obedience to the Lord's will and call. By Manny and Betty's friendship and example, they have helped to shape my life's music."

Acknowledgments

More than three decades of creating choral musicals have taught me to value the collaborative contributions of orchestrators and choral technicians. It's one thing to conceptualize a dramatic musical presentation. It's quite another to turn 10 or so songs, plus a narrative setting, over to the hands of a master musician and see the whole lifted to greatly enhanced levels of aesthetic and artistic beauty.

Wes Eby, editor of this work, has performed just such an invaluable service. Working with our submitted perspective of the Manny Chavier story, Wes has served, in effect, as an arranger, helping me to share the melodies of privately experienced blessing and faith. This book, in short, is a prosaic production, if you will, whose selected tempo, keys, lyrics, pacing, content, tone, and spiritual and philosophical design owe a great deal to the care and editing skills of my new friend and colleague. His insightful suggestions provided the creative framework for the whole. Like the finest of professional arrangers, he treated my work as his own, while adding inspiring touches of ornamentation.

Thanks, Wes, for helping me translate a story line and literary devices into the poetry of life. Your many E-mails, phone calls, letters, additions, subtractions, corrections, suggestions, and sense of mission have endeared you to my heart. You are the sort of "arranger/producer" whose commitment to excellence greatly enriches the writer's life.

—Steve Adams

Preface

Dr. Manuel Chavier* . . .

- Trained in the army as a master sergeant with a background in radio and communications.
- Received the Bronze Star Medal for heroism in the Battle of the Bulge in the European theater during World War II.
- Graduated with honors from two Christian colleges, earning two separate undergraduate degrees in theology.
- Served 10 years in the New Bedford, Massachusetts, public school system, where he was English department chairman as well as developer of seventh grade English curriculum for the city.
- Was presented an honorary doctor of divinity degree from Eastern Nazarene College in Wollaston, Massachusetts.
- Married Elizabeth McKenney, and they became parents of two children—a daughter, Ruth Gomes, and a son, Manuel Jr., both in full-time Christian service.

Rev. Chavier, a second-generation Cape Verdean American, answered God's call to become a minister to his own people in the historic fishing port of New Bedford, Massachusetts. Manuel, af-

---

*A guide on page 96 provides pronunciation of unfamiliar words in this book.

fectionately known as Manny, became one of the city's most preeminent, respected, and supported citizens.

This is the dramatic-but-true story of one couple's faith and remarkable obedience to a God-given vision. Manny Chavier, Nazarene clergyman, has positively impacted the social, moral, political, educational, and spiritual fabric of his community as few men ever do.

Working on this book has been one of the most rewarding projects of my life. I have come face-to-face with the possibility of an extended miracle. Its unfolding revelation has served to refresh my belief in human goodness while reminding me that the prayers of God's people *do* have the power to move the very mind of God.

The narrative is reminiscent of ancient biblical epics that depict the Lord's intervention in the affairs of humankind. Here is a modern-day Moses, leading an oppressed people from the slavery of ritual theocracy to the promised land of spiritual rebirth. Here are Red Seas to be crossed and desert sands to be traversed. Here, too, are cloud-by-day and fire-by-night provisions of grace—enough to leave you with a sense of awe and an openness to the work of the divinely supernatural in your own life.

Whenever helpful, I have let the Chaviers tell their own story. Direct quotes are derived from more than 27 hours of tape-recorded interviews conducted in their home in April 1999, which produced over 90-plus pages of single-space manuscript.

I can vouch for the authenticity of every detailed vignette, for New Bedford was once my hometown. Many of the events chronicled in these pages have been documented by firsthand observation and experience. My dad, brother, and I even sang, more than once, for the formative Cape Verdean Bible Conference. The heroes of this history are my friends. Each occurrence described in the pages that follow is—to written documentary, in a reverse sort of way—what the actual log book of Herman Melville's 1841 voyage on the *Acushnet* was to his subsequent literary classic *Moby Dick*.

I personally watched a couple's dream and prayers result in a basement mission with a focus limited to one city's Cape Verdean culture and population. I observed as it grew to a large evangelical church, located on a $2.5 million campus, with truly international influence, representing a diversity of multicultural traditions, needs, and nationalities. And I've seen, firsthand, a friend contribute more than a half century of his life to profound civic service.

This is no ordinary *biography*, for Manuel Chavier is no ordinary *man*. My own song owes much to the poetry of Manny's example.

—Steve Adams

Map

Introduction

A Dead Whale or a Stove Boat*

The cold Atlantic bears down upon the New England coastline with fierce, relentless unpredictability. Weather advisories of gale-force winds are heeded by old salts who know the ways of the ocean, especially those who spend most of their lives on it. In New Bedford, Massachusetts, the one-time whaling capital of the world, experienced captains and crewmen alike cast wary, leathery eyes toward the skies when forecasts call for heavy seas. More than one boat-ravaging "nor'easter" has been spawned elsewhere, only to ride the ocean crests all the way to this Gateway to Cape Cod. More than one fisherman has put out to sea from the New Bedford docks, never to return.

More than a century ago, the wives of well-to-do sea merchants spent many an anxious hour, peering through long, brass telescopes out the windows of small cupolas built into and above the attics of their clapboard-covered homes. To this day, these quaint houses line County Street atop the steep hill that looks down over picturesque Acushnet River and the harbor. Scanning that horizontal line where sea meets sky, family members searched

---

Stove boat refers to a whaling vessel that was broken or split in half by a whale. Consequently, sailors were unable to kill the mammoth animal.

day after day for the familiar, unfurled masts whose wind-driven power would bring their husbands, brothers, and dads back home after voyages that sometimes lasted three or four years. Widow's walks, these rooftop cubicles are called. And for good reason.

New Bedford was one of the busiest seaports on the globe in the 1800s. Certainly it was one of the richest. By the 1850s it was the oil capital of the entire world. A large majority of the American fleet of over 700 whaling vessels, manned by 18,000 men, set sail from this one port on voyages to Europe, Asia, the South Pacific, and the western Arctic. These adventurers hunted humpback, sperm, right, bowhead, and gray whales that skilled and fearless seafarers harpooned from tiny longboats as they rowed silently alongside their unsuspecting prey.

Many of New Bedford's bravest men took "the Nantucket sleigh ride" as handheld lances and harpoons found their marks and the giant leviathans reacted with frenzied attempts to escape the knives of would-be blubber and baleen carvers. The 30-foot whaleboats plowed through ocean swells at breathtaking speeds, as first mate and crew held on for their very lives. Once injured, sometimes the monsters—some 70 feet long and 65 tons in weight—would sound, diving deeply and towing their hunters' crafts and passengers to watery graves.

As early as the 1830s, whale oil lamps burned brightly in homes on every continent, and smokeless, odorless, long-lasting candles were lit around the globe—all because Portuguese, Cape Verdean,

Caucasian, Azorean, and African-American sailors weighed anchor from New Bedford's wharves. More whaling voyagers left New Bedford's docks in the 1850s than out of all the other seaports of the world combined. And enough square riggers came back to this singular port, their holds brimming with sperm oil, to light up the world. Whale blubber had been rendered into oil, by a high-temperature process known as *trying out*, on board the ships while at sea. Indeed, by 1860 the Industrial Revolution and the petroleum alternatives it produced were fueled in scientists' imaginations by the valiant determination and heroic deeds of New Bedford's whalers.

What old-fashioned Yankee perseverance and determination! It's New England's "right stuff."

"A dead whale or a stove boat" reads the eulogy to New Bedford's maritime-lost, which is inscribed on a huge bronze statue of a seaman, standing in the prow of a boat, harpoon poised for strike. The memorial, located in front of the downtown library, reflects the attitude of the 19th-century seafarer: "Either we come back with our cargo of whale oil, or we die going after it. The world need not lie in darkness; we're willing to risk our lives to

Monument to New Bedford's seafarers

provide light." What old-fashioned Yankee perse-verance and determination! It's New England's "right stuff."

I have walked the narrow, cobblestone streets of New Bedford's Historic National Park and have heard Herman Melville's description of the city, as he knew it in the 1800s, ringing in my ears: "The town itself is perhaps the dearest place to live in, in all New England. . . . All these brave houses and flowery gardens came from the Atlantic, Pacific, and Indian Oceans. One and all, they were harpooned and dragged up hither from the bottom of the sea" (Moby Dick).

New Bedford was, in its origins, a fishing village with sailors, tradesmen, and craftsmen drawn from every quarter of the globe by the lure of prosperity-through-whaling ventures. "Right and left, the streets take you waterward. . . . Posted like silent sentinels all around the town, stand thousands upon thousands of mortal men fixed in ocean reveries" (Moby Dick).

I have often joined these inlanders in their aquatic musings. When I return to our home in Nashville, the pungent smell of lobster, shrimp, haddock, cod, flounder, mackerel, clams, quahogs, and scallops pierces my memory, time and time again. I am drawn, in backward glances, to the waterfront where, as a boy, I attended the largest scallop festival in the world. I recall with clarity the city's celebration when actor Gregory Peck filmed the movie, Moby Dick. Mom and Dad took Nate and me to the New Bedford Hotel to eat actual whale meat, which tasted a lot like roast beef with a similar consistency. In my mind's eye, I revisit the piers of the fishing fleet. I can still see the fishermen, mending huge nets and building lobster traps. I remember catching my own prize-winning flounder on the Captain Leroy, my favorite commercial trawler, in half-day trips out to sea with my dad and brother. And I stand, once again, inside the famous Whaling Museum, gazing at an actual gigantic skeleton of a captured whale; the fabulous scrimshaw collections and nautical paintings; and the

17

Ships in New Bedford's harbor

Lagoda, *an 89-foot, half-scale replica of an old-time, square-rigged whaling bark. Marveling at its small size, I try to picture what it was like to plow the world's seas in such a relatively minuscule vessel in hunt of an adult behemoth, large enough to swallow a fleeing prophet! Across the street, I enter Seaman's Bethel and view the chapel in which Melville actually worshiped and in whose ship's-bow-shaped pulpit the novelist's Father Mapple delivered his memorable exegesis on the life and times of Jonah.*

Sooner or later my mind turns to the Nazarene parsonage on State Street, only a matter of blocks from the ocean, where we lived. How I loved to lie in a warm bed on stormy days and listen to the early morning moans of foghorns. New Bedford became my home from seventh grade through my ju-

nior year in high school when my parents, Nathan A. Adams Jr. and Mary Adams, pastored First Church of the Nazarene.

The year was 1955. I didn't realize it at the time, but our "sister church" in New Bedford had launched, six years earlier, a ministry destined to bring spiritual light to multiple thousands of people on New England's "stern and rockbound coast." Through the vision, hard work, confident faith, and unswerving determination of Pastor and Mrs. Manuel Chavier, New Bedford would, once again, become a center of global influence. The International Church of the Nazarene (formerly First Portuguese) in New Bedford, which they started, has grown over the past 40 years to be a spiritual lighthouse, beaming "the Light of the world" around the world.

This, really, is the story of one remarkable and dedicated couple, Manuel and Elizabeth Chavier (Manny and Betty to closest friends), and their labor of love in a city of approximately 100,000 souls. *Miraculous* is the only word that seems appropriate to describe what has taken place in the inner-city ministry of this unique husband-and-wife team and the Nazarenes who worship with them on Pleasant Street.

Several decades ago, Manuel and Betty Chavier said to themselves, "We will bring the Light to the world around us, or we will risk our very lives doing so."

"A dead whale or a stove boat." Ancient mariners would be proud.

PART ONE

"If My People . . . Shall Humble Themselves and Pray"

I It Can't Be Done: Attempting the Impossible

> "For mortals it is impossible, but for God
> all things are possible" (Matthew 19:26, NRSV).

Northeasterners say you haven't really driven until you've safely wheeled your car through the spaghetti-like streets and busy intersections of New York or Boston. It may likewise be true that you haven't really pastored an American, evangelical, Protestant church until you've done so in New England.

New Englanders are unique. They like tradition. They appreciate time-honored legacies. They can be slow to accept outsiders. They sometimes turn the wheels of progress by hand, an inch at a time. They know the value of the "dollah" and keep their pennies close to home. These Northeasterners are a ruddy people, used to harsh climate, fierce storms, gale winds, and six-foot snowbanks in the winter. They like their iced coffee, frappes, sodas, fish stews, raw oysters, clambakes, and clam "chowda," while sometimes resisting change, whether recipes, ideas, or methods.

For some of the above reasons, growing a church in New England during the '30s, '40s, and '50s presented challenges, to put it mildly, to evangelicals. More than one pastor, fresh out of college or from some other part of the country, found it hard to convince his congregation that the *status quo* wasn't something to "quo" about!

More than one pastor found it hard to convince his congregation that the *status quo* wasn't something to "quo" about!

Part of the reason for this conservative, evangelical mind-set was cultural. Well over three-fourths of the population in New Bedford in the 1950s was Roman Catholic by birth, personal assent, theological bias, and/or sociological perspective.

The first day of my schooling there, I was the only student in my class to complete the Lord's Prayer aloud. (Yes, school prayers were permitted in those days.) I'll never forget how all my peers suddenly stopped with the words "but deliver us from evil." I, alone, in full, conscientious voice extolled the virtues of "the kingdom, and the power, and the glory." I wanted to disappear—forever and ever. Amen. My playmates, schoolmates, next-door neighbors, grocer, dentist, physician, mechanic, teachers, and principal were, for the most part, Roman Catholic in

*thinking and orientation. The majority were greatly
admired; many became lifelong friends.*

In those days, in the minds of some, there were
huge emotional walls to be scaled on both sides of
the religious fence. In such demographic conditions, life for protestant evangelicals could be that
of a distinct minority, and for pastors desiring sub-
stantial increases in church membership and outreach, the situation often resulted in low expecta-
tions and even lower results.

*If I heard it once, I heard it a thousand times as
a teenager, "It can't be done—at least easily—in
New England." (Not exactly a motto for church-
growth strategists!)*

*The fact is that Nazarene churches on the New
England District, in those days, tended to start
small—and remain small. Dad pastored the fifth
largest Nazarene Church in six states, and it aver-
aged no more than 200. The nearest college church
had difficulty reaching above 300. In the minds of
many, large evangelical churches were next to im-
possible to grow.*

Fast-forward to the new millennium. Tour the
present, five-building, downtown campus of International Church of the Nazarene in New Bedford.
Sit in its capacity-filled, 500-seat sanctuary in either
of two services on any given Sunday morning and
hear its multicultural congregation and superb
choir sing, accompanied by organ, piano, and or-
chestra. Walk through the 200-seat chapel next
door, or the brand-new Communications Center, or
the Sunday School facilities, or the 325-seat Fellow-

24

Dr. Manuel and Betty Chavier in front of International Church of the Nazarene.

ship Hall. Visit the two church parsonages. And you'll soon see that "can't be done" is *not* one of the languages Manny Chavier speaks!

Here is a man who taps into Scriptural promise.

2   A Barrage of Tomatoes: Pioneering with Prayer

"If my people . . . shall humble themselves, and pray"
(2 Chronicles 7:14, KJV).

Prayer-Led Pioneers

That Manuel Chavier would answer God's call to carve out a new frontier of evangelical, multicultural ministry in a land where it had never been tried is no accident. A servant by heart and a pioneer by necessity, Manny was not far removed from the Pilgrim spirit. Men and women of uncommon faith and valor had set foot on Plymouth Rock, just 45 miles away, long before the waters beside present-day New Bedford had seen their first whaling ship.

If these forefathers refused to set foot in the New World until they had first signed their names to and staked their honor on the Mayflower Compact, Rev. Chavier would not attempt to claim New Bedford for Christ without a prior commitment to *prayer*. It is safe to say that dependence on God, through direct communication with Him, would be this future pastor's charter.

Scripture-Based Prayer

The first time I heard Rev. Chavier speak publicly, I was a 12-year-old seventh grader. Yet his words still echo through my mind. Preaching passionately to his people in the congregation's new basement church, he asked them to repeat with him, by memory, 2 Chronicles 7:14: "If my people, which are called by my name, shall humble themselves, and pray, and seek my face, and turn from their wicked ways; then will I hear from heaven, and will forgive their sin, and will heal their land" (KJV).

That was 43 years ago. Just recently I had the opportunity of being in Manny's church again. Not surprisingly, I found him leading his congregation in recital of this very same promise: "If my people . . . shall humble themselves, and pray . . ."

Long ago Manuel and Elizabeth Chavier signed their names to a "biblical compact." They agreed to let the Lord lead, guide, and direct their least efforts for the Kingdom, understanding that a listening God would keep His Word and intervene, when necessary, on behalf of His interceding servants.

"I always remind my people that God has a special way of working through His promises," Dr. Chavier explains. "First, He offers a precept; then, He follows with a promise. If we humble ourselves, pray, seek, and turn—that's our part—God hears, forgives, and heals—that's His part. All of God's promises are couched in this rhythm."

Manny and Betty Chavier heeded the biblically chronicled precept, which they so loved, and expected the promises to be fulfilled.

Mother-Influenced Prayer

Just as his dad's influence helped shape Pastor Chavier's lifelong work ethic, so, too, was his devout prayer life, his total dependence on the Lord, developed as a lifestyle and habit by watching his mother in the home. Mary Chavier was a saint, one of those rare Christians who breathes the ether of childlike faith.

"Mother was not educated," Manny says. "She could neither read nor write. Her whole life was built, strengthened, and developed in the posture of prayer. She had a simple faith. She prayed everything in and everything out. She was very certain about things, praying till she reached heaven. Nothing external seemed to disturb her inner peace, for she had a relationship with the Lord that transcended circumstances."

~~~~~~~~

Prayer is Manuel Chavier's "dialect."

~~~~~~~~

Like mother, like son. Manuel Chavier is a man of quiet confidence with a Yankee resolve, steely determination, and trusting faith. He is truly in tune with his times and in touch with the Lord. Because of his upbringing, he readily admits, "Like breath to my body, prayer became my life in the Lord."

Prayer is Manuel Chavier's "dialect." Never assuming a career-affiliated, stained-glass voice, Rev. Chavier prays all day long. His prayers are conversational, not strained. He begins his day with prayer. He doesn't leave his home without prayer. He prays before driving his car down the road. He prays on the way to the store. He prays at home with his family. He prays with parishioners on the phone. He prays at the church office. He prays with his doctors, his dentist, his bankers, the many business people with whom he deals every day. In short, he lives in the Presence. Prayer is as natural to this church leader as breathing. His mother's habit has become his own. Her faith, he shares. Her Lord, he knows. And just as intimately.

Manuel Chavier's commitment to the Lord is not so much contractual as communal. It is based on an active, close, and personal relationship.

A Prayer-Defined Ministry

In the army during his private devotions, Manny began to hear God speak to him about ministry. The call gradually became clarified as the Lord revealed to Manny that he was needed as a minister—a type of "missionary"—to an American city on Cape Cod.

"This is—and has been—a mission," Manny

Manny Chavier in Germany during World War II.

insists. "I have always had a 'missionary's' heart, and the Lord called me to New Bedford as definitely as He calls others to foreign fields."

This, he knew, was not a path to financial independence, not a way out of the social circles in which so many friends and relatives had been forced to live. "God saw that, in my mind and heart, at first I had no desire to be a 'missionary.' I'd had all I'd wanted of primitive living. I'd known what it was like to use a broomstick as agitator for our washing machine when I wanted clean clothes. I'd eaten with ants!"

But Manny had an obedient heart. "As an enlisted man in the military, I had sensed God's definite call to ministry. Now, in a missionary conference in Wenham, Massachusetts, at Gordon

College, I was hearing God's undeniable call to a specific mission field, New Bedford. That's when I learned the meaning of the term *sanctification*. I had to find that place of entire consecration. Just as repentance preceded my conversion, so consecration preceded my sanctification. At last, I was Christ's completely. He wanted that. I said 'yes' to His will. Then, there was none of me . . . and all of Him!" Poverty of spirit was making this servant teachable.

"When God said He wanted me to go to New Bedford, I couldn't believe it," Manny continues. "But I was willing to obey. I didn't want to tempt God, but I threw out a fleece in response to the call I was feeling. I simply wanted assurance and verification that a lifetime of ministry in New Bedford was what He wanted for me. The fleece came back to me, proven, almost immediately. I threw out a second one. Once again, God made His will crystal clear. I had no choice but to go. My call to New Bedford was confirmed on my knees."

In 1948, Adelina Domingues of New Bedford was praying earnestly. Her plea was that the Lord would send someone to help her minister to the Portuguese Cape Verdeans in the area. Cape Verdeans had settled in New Bedford by the thousands. The migration from the old country, some 3,000 miles away off the northwest coast of Africa, had begun in whaling days. They had come as a great seafaring people in search of adventure. While back in the Islands, many had gone on whale and shark hunts. Now they sought employment in a more prosperous land.

Dr. Chavier describes the people among whom God had called Mrs. Domingues and him to minister. "Many transplanted Cape Verdeans have stories similar to that of my father, John Chavier. His cousin was captain of a ship, and Dad worked his way from the Cape Verde Islands to the United States aboard that boat. Immigration laws were more relaxed in those days. Dad was able to walk off the vessel onto American soil. With the help of friends, he found jobs in the Lincoln and Central Falls, Rhode Island area, which was north of Providence. These neighborhoods were so new to him that he had to mark street posts with chalk so he could find his way home again.

"To support his family, Dad worked two shifts in sweat shops for 13 years. With only six months of formal education in his homeland, the man was self-taught. He was so poor when he arrived in America that he borrowed the first quarter he ever had.

"In those days, there were only two classes of people in Cape Verde—the rich and poor, with very little in between. People born there didn't have easy lives. Compared to the standard of living in the States, the Islands had much less to offer. American supermarkets, for example, dazzled Cape Verdeans. Conveniences didn't exist back home. Electric power could be turned off at any moment. The beautiful cars to drive and gasoline offered at every other corner here in the United States were inconceivable there.

"Historically, the Cape Verde Islands, a colony of Portugal, became a place to which the mother country—once a great maritime power—sent political prisoners. These were intelligent people who simply had run across the grain of the politics of the day. It was much like Russian leaders sending dissidents to Siberia.

"Even though the name Cape Verde literally means 'a place that is green,' it is not. Our fatherland is quite arid and dry. Water comes from the sea via large desalination plants. The winds of the Sahara Desert in northern Africa blow across that part of the globe and seriously affect the Islands, leaving them extremely parched. Though the Islands, a product of volcanic eruptions, are fertile, there are few, if any, major industries. The natives' way of life has been agricultural and aquatic. The country has, unfortunately, been beset by third-world poverty."

The Cape Verdean legacy, then, is one of subservience. Descendants of the Islands are somewhat disdainfully referred to as Cape Verdeans, rather than Portuguese, to distinguish them from their European counterparts. Continental Portuguese, spoken in Island schools and churches, was the official written language. But Cape Verdeans, including Manny, learned to speak Creole, the idiom of the streets, in the home long before they spoke English.

"Cape Verde is a nationality unto itself, to some degree, even though it is tied to Portugal," Pastor Chavier continues. "The culture that one finds in the Cape Verde Islands is very much a blend of nationalities. Some of my relatives, for example, had Italian blood; others, French. That's typical of the Cape Verdean families and why you see people's names here in New Bedford with hints of so many cultural backgrounds. There's such a mix of blood strains."

Cape Verdeans have been held at a distance by some of their Portuguese brothers and sisters. "You'll find that some Portuguese have always considered the Cape Verdeans to be a different class," Manny says. "For example, our people aren't often invited to join the Portuguese-American clubs you see in this area. Even though Cape Verdeans go to Portugal, as Americans go to Florida to enjoy the beaches, and even though many of the people (intelligent dissidents) have become doctors, etc., affluent professionals among native Islanders are still a cultural minority. If you came from the right class of Cape Verdeans, you could more likely flow into upward levels of society. Otherwise, you were sort of handed down tidbits of the Portuguese culture. (Whatever television Cape Verdeans had, for instance, came from Portugal and the Azores.)"

These, then, were the people whom Mrs. Domingues held in her heart. In particular, she dreamed of helping them break free of the spiritual chains with which the old country's theocracy had bound them. She shared her vision with Abel Azevedo, pastor of the Portuguese Calvary Baptist Church of Lonsdale, Rhode Island, just north of Providence. Mrs. Domingues heard her friend tell, in glowing terms, about one of his former Sunday School pupils, Manuel Chavier. Rev. Azevedo suggested that Mrs. Domingues invite the young Chavier to speak to the group of her friends with whom she and Pastor Azevedo regularly met on Sunday afternoons.

~~~~~

Soon the tiny congregation voted to ask Manuel Chavier to become their first pastor. He consented.

~~~~~

In the meantime, the missions conference was being conducted at Gordon College. Rev. Chavier was challenged there to surrender his life to be a missionary to some foreign country, he thought. Little did he realize that the Lord was calling him into selfless ministry at the same time New Bedford Cape Verdeans were praying for a leader.

When Rev. Chavier received Mrs. Domingues's invitation to preach in New Bedford, he accepted, not knowing that he and the New Bedfordites would fall in love with each other immediately. Soon the tiny congregation voted to ask Manuel Chavier to become their first pastor. He consented.

A Divinely Assigned Mission

So it was that, with a prayer in his heart, the 27-year-old Manuel Chavier, a college junior, answered God's calling on his life. He had been practicing his preaching in high school auditoriums all over the Northeast, in soup kitchens and inner-city missions, on Boston's busy street corners, and in jails.

In April 1948, driving the 60 miles from Massachusetts's capital, this single, handsome, young theology major was ready to accept a pastoral role in the "mission" field to which God had led him. He would start a church from scratch. The Lord had brought him to this very moment and would provide both wisdom and resources. Decades later, an article in New Bedford's *Standard-Times* newspapers would reflect that Manuel Chavier arrived at his divinely appointed ministry with but "one tangible asset: *faith.*"

Turning off of Cape Cod's Route 6, Manny passed vast enclaves of multistoried textile mills and headed toward New Bedford's waterfront district. The 19-mile-square city stretches out like an elongated ship, its coastline protected from the Atlantic by a natural harbor, a massive stone jetty constructed by the Corps of Engineers, and the guardian care of majestic, caisson-style Butler's Flat Lighthouse. Rev. Chavier drove his '36 DeSoto past huge fishing canneries, auction houses, and fleets of commercial trawlers. He passed dock after dock of coast guard vessels, cargo ships, ferries, draggers, scallopers, and older barks, brigs, and schooners. The young man saw marine gear piled high, mountains of lobster pots, ornate mastheads, massive steel nets, and towering cranes used for loading and unloading mysterious cargoes. Seagulls congregated noisily on the piers and circled overhead. Interspersed along the wharfs were many saloons frequented by thirsty dockworkers and sailors.

Seaside activities filled Manny's field of vision on the left. A bustling center of commerce emerged on the right, replete with banks, city offices, a library, a post office, and one of the oldest continuously operated United States Customs Houses in America. Higher up on the hill he noted old mariners' houses, bedecked with an occasional boxwood rose garden or a historic wooden pergola. And everywhere he observed assorted stores, shops, inns, and eating establishments.

Manny breathed in the salty air pungent with seaweed, chopped bait, and fish oil. Navigating his car without compass down one-way, one-lane streets, which were once lit at dusk with whale oil lamps, he found a parking place near the Lady of Assumption Church and began knocking on residential doors. *Here I will start my evangelistic outreach*, he decided, as he looked around at row after row of three- and four-story tenement houses, apartment-laden housing projects, and the narrow, gabled, private dwellings—covered with rust-colored, weathered, clapboard siding—that fishers and textile workers called "home."

If he had wanted an inner-city ministry, he had definitely come to the right place. Cars, bikes, and people all jostled for ownership of every square foot of space in this maritime melting pot of disparate cultures. It seemed as if incoming tides had carried a miniaturized Europe to America's doorstep and laid it out, all over again, in a patchwork quilt of customs and languages, narrow lanes and architectural designs, antiques and signs. Here, too,

Asia, the East Indies, and South Pacific embraced the New World. In New Bedford, history brooded, while "future shock" tried feverishly to connect to it.

Door-to-Door Canvassing

Manuel Chavier was ready for aggressive ministry. After all, he had earned a Bronze Star in the Battle of the Bulge during World War II, had supervised more than 500 men at once in complex military assignments, and had definitely learned to take the offense. Leadership training in the army had prepared this soldier of the Cross to face the unknown with quiet courage and resolve. As previously observed, the old work ethic, espoused by his father, was coming into play. If energy spent could make a difference, Manny was ready to pound the pavement.

One of the very first apartment doors on which the God-called pastor knocked yielded a willing audience. The man of the house was severely ill and welcomed Manny inside to minister. It was an auspicious beginning.

Street Corner Evangelism

Weeks went by. At first, Manuel Chavier held Sunday services in various homes. Then, for one winter, afternoon meetings were conducted in a Methodist Church on Allen Street provided by a friend, Rev. William Moseley. Finally, the congregation rented a facility, the Odd Fellows Hall on Sixth

Street, which the church was able to obtain at the weekly rate of $5 for two hours. During this period, the young minister visited many of the community's neighborhoods and gradually learned the cultural lay of the land. Desiring to "fish the right waters" for the Lord, he prayed continually for guidance as he moved by God's direction into those areas where Cape Verdeans most often assembled socially.

Noting continuous gatherings at the playground in Joseph Monte Park on the south edge of town, Rev. Chavier had tried door-to-door evangelism; now it was time for a new approach. Rigging up a turntable, loudspeaker, and bullhorn to his car battery, Manny parked near an area in the park known as "the wall." Men frequently hid behind this concrete structure to gamble with dice, and it was the site of many other activities, both lawful and illegal. The would-be pastor, with previously obtained permission of appropriate authorities, then cranked up his PA system and played recorded music to attract attention. With a boldness born both of youth and the Holy Spirit's empowerment, he proceeded to preach fiery, anointed messages.

Crowds gathered. Some mocked or jeered, taunting, "Who do you think you are? You're just a kid!" Others listened cautiously. Many neighbors sat on their upper-story windowsills and watched from afar.

The Lord blessed this young, street-corner preacher's efforts. He repeated the visits every Sunday afternoon after conducting morning services at the Odd Fellows Hall location. People were being saved in New Bedford, right there by "the wall." Not many feet away, the Roman Catholic hierarchy stood nearby observing.

A Prayer-Provided Miracle

Manny longed for a better auditorium in which to hold more formal meetings, especially a Sunday School. One day near Joseph Monte Park, he noticed a large building whose window shutters were tightly closed. The aspiring pastor got out of his car and walked around the Acushnet Avenue property, inspecting its potential. *Could this place be empty and available?* he wondered.

Suddenly, he heard a voice. "What are you looking for, mister?" An older lady was watching his every move, as if a self-appointed guardian of the edifice.

"Who owns this building?" Pastor Chavier inquired, as he proceeded to explain his situation.

"This is a gambling hall!" the woman almost shouted. "It's used constantly. My son owns it. He lives in Providence, but I doubt that he'd rent it to anyone."

Not being one to take no for an answer easily, Manny wrote down the owner's Rhode Island address, climbed back into his car, and set out to find the woman's offspring. Two hours later, he stood in front of the "entrepreneur's" house, conversing with the man face-to-face. With more zeal than intellect (by his own admission), Rev. Chavier said, "I was just talking to your mother, and she told me you're running a business in your New Bedford location. I was wondering if you'd close down for a week and let me use it for a series of meetings."

The gentleman, naturally, declined the idea of shutting down his lucrative enterprise. Manny wouldn't give up. Asking if he could have a few minutes of the stranger's time, he proceeded to detail for a whole hour how the Lord had called him to New Bedford and exactly why he had made the trip to the man's home. When Manny had finished, much to his amazement, the gentleman agreed, "OK, I'll close down." Just like that!

Manny went back to New Bedford, excited and ready. He cleaned up the hall and opened its windows to the light of day. Coaxing some girls to play the piano, he advertised the meetings and moved furniture in for the occasion.

Right after Labor Day, he began a series of evening services. The people thought it was a county fair. They filled every seat inside and sat on the fences nearby.

For two nights, everything went superbly well, even though Roman Catholic priests could see what was going on from their church steps. On the third or fourth night, however, some boys visited the scene with a premeditated plan and bags of tomatoes. At a given signal, they started flinging their squishy grenades, showering Manny and everyone near him. The people in attendance scattered all over the place.

The young minister knew the attack had been orchestrated. His immediate reaction was to go home and let the "barbarians" have their way. Instead, he got down on his knees together with

Adelina Domingues and Irene Jones, the two others who had stayed, and prayed. The Lord told him not to let these threats put an end to the services.

The next night, the evangelicals opened the doors to another full house. Manny preached with anointing. This time, when he gave an invitation, 20 individuals came forward to receive Christ, including—believe it or not!—the mother of the man who owned the hall. She was gloriously saved.

The next Sunday, after a terrific week of meetings, Manny went back to the building's owner and asked him to close down every Sunday afternoon so Manny could hold a Sunday School on the premises. Again, miraculously, the man agreed. That is, until he found out he was losing too much business. He then insisted on using the upstairs for his gambling operation, while downstairs Christians were singing "O How I Love Jesus." Dr. Chavier likes to say, "The devil was on top, and we were on the bottom!"

The Lord then intervened more permanently. Due to a sudden change in the political climate, the gambling business came to an abrupt end. The owner of the hall searched out Pastor Chavier and announced, "You can have the whole building!"

This meant that Sunday School could be held upstairs. For $30 a month, the group of 20 or so believers was able to move in.

3

Wharf Rats and Death Threats: Accepting the Challenge

"The prayer of the righteous is powerful and effective" (James 5:16, NRSV).

A Prayer-Seasoned Church

The small group of Cape Verdean believers, who had once been pelted with tomatoes, now met regularly on Acushnet Avenue. This fellowship of obedient disciples continued to heed the Lord's admonition to pray and seek His face. "The new building was a strategic answer to prayer for us," Pastor Chavier declares. "It was located where the Cape Verdeans lived.

"I soon came to learn that there are two legs by which Christians walk this journey: one, the Word; and, two, prayer. One without the other means trouble. Prayer without the Word can lead to fanaticism. And the Word without prayer can lead to legalism. The two have to be properly seasoned.

They flow together. I brought these lessons to the work that God had given to me."

Leaning on prayer and Scriptures, such as 2 Chronicles 7:14, the would-be minister gradually became "Pastor" Chavier.

A Vision-Sharing Mate

Manny was fortunate, for he wouldn't have long to minister in this new town alone. The Lord had been preparing a missions-minded spouse for him, someone who would share both his life and heartfelt call to ministry.

Elizabeth G. McKenney also attended Gordon College. The daughter of a Baptist minister from Everett, Massachusetts, Betty had majored in theology with a minor in music. In her mind, she hoped to be a missionary to South America.

The Lord—and Manuel Chavier—had other plans for her. Manny pursued this talented girl for two years and eight months. "I didn't have a chance! Mother prayed Betty into my life!" He remembers. "She told me this girl was different, in a positive way, from all the others." Mary Chavier stayed on her knees until her son got down on his to propose to Miss McKenney.

On August 18, 1950, Manny and Betty were married. The newlyweds moved into rooms in two consecutive homes of friends until they were able to set up housekeeping in their own apartment about six months later.

From the beginning, Betty Chavier graced her

Manny and Betty Chavier at their wedding reception.

role as "parsonage queen." And the fact that she just happened to be an accomplished musician and organist with additional training at the Boston Conservatory didn't hurt her husband's ministry any.

A Less-than-Ideal Parsonage

Life at 117 Grinnell Street wasn't easy for the happy couple. The church was by no means large enough to pay adequate compensation to its pastor. At first, the congregation gave the Chaviers $10 a week; then the salary was upped to $25. And there was no official parsonage. Manny and Betty lived in five rooms on the first floor of a three-story tenement house in what they describe as a ghetto area of the city.

"We were near the ocean, so wharf rats visited us!" Betty recalls. "Lots of them! We're talking huge rodents! In our home! Many nights, I'd hear noises under our bed. Manuel would have to grab a bucket and push a rat or two into it before taking a hammer to their heads." (Manny remembers setting traps; Betty recalls the hammer method.)

The Chavier's daughter, Ruth, with her husband, Rev. Edmund Gomes, and their children, Joshua and Priscilla.

The Chavier's son, J. R., a Nazarene minister, with daughter, Jessica; wife, Almeda; and daughter, Monica.

"When our first baby, Ruthie, came along," Betty continues, "I was always petrified that a rat would find her crib. Other renters in the same tenement brought cockroaches and immoral lifestyles. I kept wondering, *When are we going to get out of this place?* We certainly were "missionaries.""

Life-Threatening Incidents

The young groom himself was not without some misgivings about personal safety. "Two clergymen of another religious persuasion didn't like what they saw happening in our church," Manny says. "Our congregation was growing too swiftly to suit them. They started harassing me in various ways on a daily basis."

The men followed Manny wherever he went in their neighborhood, shadowing his every move. When he confronted them face-to-face, they threatened to take him to court for proselytizing. He replied, "Give us the date, and, by God's grace, we'll be there." Dr. Chavier proceeded to share his perspective of the gospel with them, refusing to back down. Convicted by the truth, they fled.

With the passing of time, pressure from local ecclesiastical sources increased until Manny's life was threatened. "The day actually arrived, when one of their laypeople came to me, looked me straight in the eye, and said, 'I'll kill you!'" Manny remembers.

"I replied, 'I love you.' You see, I had learned that we're not called to survive; we're called to serve. Surviving was not my problem. God had showed me that. It's so wonderful to see how the Lord stands by His servants. That same night, someone stoned one of our church buildings. From that point on, I had to watch myself all the time. Non-evangelical opposition was strong!"

A God-Inspired Invitation

In the early days of Manny's ministry, Louise Robinson Chapman, wife of then-General Superintendent J. B. Chapman, was president of the Women's Foreign Missionary Society (now Nazarene World Mission Society). She learned about the work of Manuel Chavier from Major Casey, a well-to-do layman from New Bedford First Church. When a speaking engagement for which she was scheduled was unexpectedly canceled, Mrs. Chapman found herself with free time. Mr. Casey took her to meet Manuel Chavier and gain a firsthand overview of the minister's dreams and activities.

"That Sunday morning when they entered our building," Dr. Chavier recalls, "I had Sunday School children in my arms. Mrs. Chapman came over to me and said, 'Brother, why don't you consider becoming a part of us?'" Mrs. Chapman then told Manny about the Nazarene mission work already established in the Cape Verde Islands.

After consulting friends, he decided to accept Mrs. Chapman's gracious invitation. He looked forward to denominational help. In February 1949,

Louise Robinson Chapman *(left)* **visiting New Bedford.** *(Left to right):* **Dr. Chapman, Dr. Chavier, and Mrs. Adelina Domingues.**

J. C. Albright, superintendent of the New England District, organized out of what had been known as the Portuguese Free Gospel Mission in New Bedford, the First Portuguese Church of the Nazarene with 23 charter members.

Christian friends, Rev. Abel Azevedo and James Azevedo, gave their wholehearted support to this work. Likewise, John Turple, pastor of the First Church of the Nazarene in New Bedford, and his people showered the newly formed Cape Verdean congregation with support. Several people from the Calvary Baptist Church in Lonsdale, Rhode Island, traveled each week, often through inclement weather, to stand by the new congregation with their presence, gifts, and talents.

A Nazarene-Ordained Minister

The school of hard knocks was not the only training ground for Manuel Chavier. He had never been one to shirk educational improvement—of any kind. Though he had left high school without graduating to help feed his family, he had gone back to school and earned a diploma after completing military service. The government had opened a high school for veterans in Pawtucket, Rhode Island. GIs were allowed to advance at their own pace. True to form, Manny managed to fulfill all requirements for two years of work in just seven months. He went through two years of algebra in the same period, covered 900 pages of history in 30 days, and passed all tests. An amazing feat!

Manny prepared to supplement his future salary as a pastor. The church wouldn't be able to pay a full-time salary for many years. "I realized that, as Paul made tents to take care of his daily needs, I would have to teach to make enough to live," he comments. "So, I purposely took education courses. I graduated with a lot more credits than I needed—rather like having a double major."

As a full-fledged pastor of a baby church in New Bedford who had agreed to associate his ministry with the Nazarene denomination, he was obliged to study Wesleyan theology. Wanting very much to gain the training from Eastern Nazarene College (ENC) as quickly as possible, he managed, against the concerned advice of Dean Bertha Munroe, to complete the Th.B. degree—comprehensives, orals, and all—in just one year.

Manuel Chavier became an ordained Nazarene minister in 1951. "Dr. Hardy Powers was the general superintendent," Manny says. "I was in the same class of ordinands as Dr. Stephen Nease, who later became president of ENC. It was he and I together! Years later, in 1985, when they honored me with a doctorate of divinity, Steve was there. We had a lot to say to each other."

Now that college was behind him, it was time for Manny Chavier to see if a decade of military, educational, and theological training would make a difference.

PART TWO

"Then Will I Hear from Heaven"

Lighthouse Evangelism: Loving People to Christ

"This is my commandment, that you love one another as I have loved you" (John 15:12, NRSV).

A Love-Cemented Church

Manuel and Betty Chavier settled into their home and went to work as a team. As educators in their community, the young couple began to make a mark for Christ outside the church. Together, they started to establish professional relationships in New Bedford that would reverberate profoundly in years to come.

The First Portuguese Church of the Nazarene was on the move. The Chaviers had more than calling and training on their side as they tackled the task of "growing a church" while working full-time, secular jobs. These two saints of God are, first and foremost, lovers of people. Their genuine, Christian love is infectious. Everything they do is bathed in prayer and the Word. But the third ingredient in their recipe for church growth is pure, old-fashioned, observable, radiant, selfless love. How else does one explain a pastor leaving his Wednesday night adult congregation in the hands of capable layleaders for many weeks, taking the church's children into his office during the midweek service, and teaching them how to pray? What other reason is there for a minister to carry in his pockets food coupons from local grocers to distribute to needy homes?

Today, many pastors and laypeople are searching for novel twists and new ideas to catch the attention of people in our contemporary culture, something that will bring folks into church. Perhaps they should look at the Chaviers' successful approach, one that focused on fundamentals and on the Christ who modeled outreach through love.

Prayer, the Scripture, and love built New Bedford's First Portuguese Church. Prayer and Scripture provided calling and guidance; love was the underlying motivation.

"Once I tell you I love you, you can put a demand on me."

Pastor Chavier expresses his love in a personalized greeting, familiar to anyone who knows him: "Has anyone told you they love you today?" You cannot be with the man one minute without hearing him ask the "love question." He poses it to everyone with whom he comes in contact. Then he hastens to add, "If not, let me be the first! I love you a hundred miles an hour, you know."

The chorus "Did Anybody Tell You?" was penned by Sharyn McNeil, wife of one of Pastor Chavier's staff members. Dr. Earl Lee, who came from New Bedford, gave the song considerable exposure to his worldwide "congregation" of thousands through the tape ministry of Pasadena, California, First Church of the Nazarene while he was pastor.

Reflecting on the tune's origins, Manny says: "The has-anybody-told-you greeting came naturally to me, for I love people. The question isn't forced. It isn't just talk. You see, once I tell you I love you, you can put a demand on me. There are some definite, important consequences to the statement. There are personal commitments made.

"I say to my people, 'Most of you can quote John 3:16; but how many of you know 1 John 3:16?' This Scripture tells us that we are to lay down our lives for others, even as Christ laid down His for us. For you and me, this is where the rubber hits the road. I should be ready to *die* for you. (Parenthetically, it's this kind of holiness that I teach.)"

Dr. Chavier knows that Christian love is something caught, not taught. "Real love is not something that I can manufacture. The Lord makes us increase in love one toward another. This is God's work. So, the closer we are to Him, the more this kind of response comes from the soul. And other people pick up on our love, or the lack thereof. We broadcast it. Love, in a leader, is like enthusiasm; it's caught by people!"

Reaching-Out Love

Manuel and Betty Chavier have taken Christ's love outside their own home and church. From the start, they shared a love for their community that found expression in three distinct areas of concern: (1) the domestic; (2) the social/educational; and (3) the spiritual.

"The Lord made it plain to me that, if we were to have an impact for Him in our community," Dr. Chavier states, "we'd have to take His love to the homes of the area, to the minds and hearts of our citizens."

The First Portuguese Church of the Nazarene would start with ministry to the family unit, reach out with social implications, and above all, present the marvelous gospel of Jesus Christ.

1. Home-Reaching Strategies

Manuel and Betty have always cared deeply about the institution of the family. Dedicated to each other and their children, Ruth (usually called Ruthie) and Manuel Jr. (better known as J. R.), they soon realized that in certain parts of New Bedford 90 percent of the youngsters were without the support of fathers. Moreover, many marriage partners were victims of spousal unfaithfulness, and in some sections of the town nuclear families were a rare exception.

Their hearts broken by what they saw, Pastor and Mrs. Chavier decided to take their message directly to the living rooms of private homes. With individual families they would try to develop pockets of influence that would gravitate to the heart, which is the Church itself. They made personal calls to members' homes a top priority. "I taught school until the middle of the afternoon. Then immediately I'd go calling in the homes," Pastor Chavier recalls. "I had people in the church help me correct students' papers and fill out some of the grading reports that needed to be entered. I maintained oversight responsibility, of course."

The "Chavier Doctrine" is that discipleship is a direct result of being with other disciples.

Next, the Chaviers instituted a series of midweek, satellite Bible studies, running as many as eight in a seven-day period. These were informal, hour-long meetings that took place in converts' homes. Members and friends would invite neighbors to their residences for prayer meetings. Pastor Chavier would then share God's Word in carefully, prayerfully prepared homilies replete with practical applications.

"Our ministry in New Bedford began in homes,"

Manny recalls. "From the very first, we designed small- and large-group settings in which our folks could experience a sort of personal intimacy. We encouraged fellowship. We planned for fellowship. When we got new people in, we gave them immediate opportunities to start relating within the body.

"God says, 'But if we walk in the light, as he is in the light, we have fellowship with one another' (1 John 1:7). Where's the light? In the Scriptures. This is a principle in which we firmly believe: From fellowship come ways in which people can minister to each other."

The "Chavier Doctrine," then, is that discipleship is a direct result of being with other disciples.

"I think I picked up on this from E. V. Hill," Manny admits. "I like to say that phase one for church growth is *salvation*—and, for Nazarenes, *sanctification*—of potential converts. Phase two is *fellowship* or *koinonia*, where believers learn how to understand and love each other. The final phase involves *good works* or doing good in Christ's name.

"The end of fellowship is discipleship. The former just naturally leads into the latter. It's a mix. Some training is direct; some, indirect. But trying to encourage the doing, without the becoming, is almost futile."

Dr. Chavier feels it is important for him to assume a leading role in these in-the-home midweek meetings, which continues to this day. "It has helped us establish a sort of universal presence throughout the city and has placed the church in people's minds," he says.

"We are constantly feeding into different geographical areas. And always, without my having to say as much, there is a subliminal message. 'See you Sunday' is my good-bye."

2. Education-Based Outreach

Having received professional degrees themselves, Manuel and Betty set out to improve the educational status of the Cape Verdeans they served. In so doing, they became two of the city's most respected educators.

Betty Chavier began her work in the public school system, first as a substitute teacher. But she soon found herself employed five days a week. She taught fifth and sixth graders for 37 years at the Robert C. Ingraham School on Rivet Street.

"Much of that time, I participated in Manuel's calling program," Betty recalls. "Every week on Tuesdays, when I wasn't teaching, I'd pick someone up, and we'd go visiting door-to-door. I wanted to show our people that they, too, could work for the Lord and maintain a career. I also went with Manuel in the church-on-the-road series of home Bible studies that were a vital part of our early mission work."

Pastor Chavier had his own commitment to intellectual excellence. "I penetrated the educational area of ministry by being a teacher myself for 10 years," he says. "The Lord helped me to do so successfully. In less than three years, I had completed a six-year master's degree English program from the State Teacher's College in Bridgewater, Massachusetts (located only about 30 miles north of New Bedford and now Bridgewater State College). As chairman of Normandin's English department, I guided the activities of eight colleagues. In addition, I developed the seventh-grade English curriculum for the city. When it finally came time for me to turn in my resignation and become a full-time pastor, my principal, Mr. Deland, didn't want to accept it. I had just received an $800 pay increase, and the school committee was willing to do more. The superintendent offered me a principalship, if I'd stay on."

I remember well passing Manny in the hallways of Normandin Junior High every day when I was in the seventh grade. His great smile—a trademark—greeted students all day long, and they loved him.

"Witnessing, you know, is not all verbal," Manny says. "A lot of it has to do with lifestyle. We're not always standing up and shouting, 'Here are the four spiritual laws!' No, we work hard, preparing the soil all around us, so that when we do sow the seed of the gospel, people will be receptive. You don't put seed in hard ground.

"I've always believed there's a soil-preparation process related to reaching the lost. There's a strategy. You don't go at it haphazardly. Others have to respect you before they will listen to you. They're looking for models—for believers who remain consistent."

Manuel and Betty Chavier have been just such spiritually exemplary models. Honored in 1969 with

**Rev. Chavier with some of his students at
Normandin Junior High School.**

the Cape Verdean Achievement Award, Dr. Chavier
was recognized by New Bedford's city fathers as an
educator-clergyman whose singular voice of acute
reason and moral courage merited their ongoing attention. As a result, he received frequent invitations
to speak or pray at school and civic functions.

3. Soul-Winning Priority

Evangelism is, and always has been, the hall-
mark of the Chaviers' mission. They are, in all and
above all, soul winners. Manny makes a point of reminding everyone of the biblical injunction, "He
that winneth souls is wise" (Proverbs 11:30, KJV).

"This verse has two related meanings to me,"
he is quick to point out. "Christians are to be com-

mended for sharing what they have experienced, and soul winners shouldn't leave their brains behind when they embark on their mission. There are techniques and methods to be mastered; there's a message to be prepared for intelligent, moving delivery; and there are needy people to be reached."

To a *Standard-Times* reporter in New Bedford, Pastor Chavier stated his mission succinctly: "I work for God. . . . In general, I find that the need of men and women in the world of business, of education, of work, and at home, is spiritual. Man, in my estimation, is a spiritual being within a body. I say that the medical doctors take care of the shell. I take care of the egg. Every need that man has, when I trace it down to its fundamentals, is a spiritual need. . . . Starting from this premise . . . I have been able to do more for my community."

Ministry to the soul is of paramount importance to this minister. "There are three questions I ask when I think about the task at hand: 'How then shall they call on him in whom they have not believed? and how shall they believe in him of whom they have not heard? and how shall they hear without a preacher?'" (Romans 10:14, KJV).

"As sovereign as God is, as great as He is, He's limited himself to you and me to do His work. As a pastor, I've learned that I'm called to be *in between*. As I follow my Master, I've discovered that He ministered between heaven and hell for my soul. Even when He hung on the Cross, there were two thieves: one stood for rejection; one, reception. Ministry always takes place in between these two choices and the two alternative destinies they represent. I am the Good Shepherd's 'under shepherd.' I stand in the gap between earth and heaven for Him."

It is this soul-winning calling that motivates every program in which the Chaviers involve themselves and their people. "There's a certain ease in Zion that people find themselves getting into, if I don't keep our soul-winning function before them constantly," Pastor Chavier declares. "We get very comfortable. We forget we're in a battle. It's not a rest camp we're in. That's what most churches are: rest camps. They've arrived at a given pinnacle, determined by numbers, as if Christ's kingdom has a price. God's not looking at our numerical or budget goals.

"The Christian's job as a soul winner is to *plant*. It's not up to us to worry about the harvest. The Lord takes care of that. He gives the increase. It's up to us to plant the seed and to water it. (That's why we still have revivals. Rev. Paul Neal, Nazarene evangelist, has been with us every other year for more than 20 times. The Lord has greatly used His ministry here.)

"Therefore, while I'm doing what I'm doing, I must be conscious that the Lord is anointing me, constantly applying what is being said. Without His involvement, it's useless.

"We're back to 2 Chronicles again, back to the basics. We have to pray, in all situations, that the Lord will give us the right words and touch us. Lives are at stake!"

Manuel Chavier feels the soul-winning imperative so strongly, he lets it drive his entire church program. "Everything we do is spiritual. Even a baseball game has to be spiritual. If it's not spiritual, it doesn't belong in the church. That's what we have that the YMCA doesn't have. If we have a Sunday School picnic, it's spiritual! No matter what we do, we're seeking the Lord's anointing.

"God is Spirit, and if we would worship Him, we must do so in spirit and in truth (John 4:24). We simply need to be about the 'Father's business.'"

Dr. Chavier is a recipient of the Brotherhood Award, which was presented by the Prince Henry Society, a group of businessmen, for "reaching out and giving . . . time to help improve the living conditions of lonely, elderly, and disadvantaged persons in the community regardless of race, color, creed or age." The highly respected Dr. Chavier, with his wife's help, *has been* about his Father's business, presenting a message of wholeness that balances spiritual ministry with social, intellectual, and physical concerns. A "total ministry for the total man."

For the Chaviers, however, the soul-winning objective predominates. How else might one account for the three-foot-tall lighthouse, standing on the right at the front of the sanctuary, that is lit every Sunday following any week in which at least one new convert has been led to Christ?

The light is usually *on!*

5

Character as Collateral: Building the Kingdom

"Unless the LORD builds the house, those who build it labor in vain" (Psalm 127:1, NRSV).

A Church Basement Facility

By 1951, the fledgling congregation of the First Portuguese Nazarene Church was much in need of its own facilities. It's hard to maintain consistent growth in undersized or temporary quarters. The challenge was not only to find a site but also to purchase it and then build a basement church—without one penny of savings! Through a miraculous series of events, Pastor Chavier was able to purchase prime real estate for $200 plus back taxes in downtown New Bedford, and pay for the property and a new building with a bank loan granted on the basis of his character alone. No collateral required!

On October 1 of the same year, Rev. C. Neal Hutchinson joined Dr. Chavier in turning over the first shovel of dirt for a church building. It was a most memorable groundbreaking service. The ministers were joined by Al Braley Sr., a carpenter, and

Manuel Grace, the first trustee of the Portuguese Church of the Nazarene and the only member ever given "trustee emeritus" status.

Subsequently, a church basement sanctuary was constructed for $28,000. The church paid off its indebtedness without ever missing a payment. The Lord had provided! As the church's "50th Anniversary" booklet puts it, "Do you see the miracle? Our collateral was in God and in the character of our pastor."

A Miracle-Provided Superstructure

Pastor Chavier knew that he would have to raise a superstructure on the basement building as

Dedication of basement church. Rev. Chavier is at the pulpit. First row on far right is Rev. Nathan Adams, the author's father, beside District Superintendent J. C. Albright.

soon as possible if he expected Cape Verdeans to look upon the Nazarene Church as more than a mission. So, after completion of the basement sanctuary, Rev. Chavier went back to see Mr. Carpenter at the Fairhaven Institution for Savings. Manny was pleased to find the newly acquired friend happy with the church's history and agreeable to the idea of loaning $50,000 for construction of the superstructure with an auditorium to seat 200.

God sent two more miracles the Chaviers' way, in the persons of Joe Dupre, mason and bricklayer, and William McKay, a most knowledgeable Christian woodworker. Mr. Dupre, laboring from June to

General Superintendent D. I. Vanderpool and Rev. Chavier at dedication of church in 1955.

Completed superstructure

November, charged the church only $3,000 to complete all masonry. Mr. McKay did the finishing carpentry work. When completed in 1955, First Portuguese Church stood proud and tall on Purchase Street, its steeple a beacon to all who might seek spiritual guidance and fellowship.

The Lord blessed the congregation in this location. In 1962, Dr. Chavier left his teaching job and became the church's full-time pastor. Attendance increased to a weekly average of 200, and a record attendance of 433 in Sunday School was set one October. The First Portuguese Church was reaching out into the community. No longer was it looked upon as a home missions enterprise.

In 1967 and 1972, Pastor Chavier saw the need for Sunday School classrooms and a youth building. Parish House One and, five years later, Parish House Two were added at the unbelievable cost of $30,000.

A Dutch-Colonial Parsonage

The Chaviers' "temporary" parsonage was a five-room apartment, complete with roaches and rodents. Here, Manny and Betty raised their children for eight years, all the time wishing for a more suitable home.

Yet, the church salary, supplemented by teachers' then-limited incomes, did little to enlarge the family's nest egg. The Chaviers prayed. They sought the Lord's assistance, as usual, on their knees.

In 1959 God gave Betty her heart's desire—a new parsonage! Manny had heard of a choice piece of property in Fairhaven, Massachusetts. With $25 in his checking account, he set out to find the owner, one Mr. Dumas. Knowing the land was worth $3,000, Dr. Chavier inquired about the price.

Mr. Dumas seemed touched by the conversation. "How about $500 for the two adjacent lots?" he replied.

Merchant's Bank loaned the young pastor $500 on his name alone. And the Lord laid it on the heart of Mr. McKay, age 79, to build the house. The Dutch-colonial home was erected for just $14,000. Its senior-citizen builder, a perfectionist, climbed rafters and rooflines like a young man. He finished the basement the following winter, allowing Manny to pay for the work over time. In 1969 at age 87, Mr. McKay put up a two-car garage for the Chaviers for $2,000.

Dr. Chavier drove every Wednesday morning for 22 years to a "mission field" on the docks.

"I always say this should be a lesson in refusing to put old-timers out to pasture," Manny declares. "Here I am, pastoring in my late 70s. Mr. McKay built a new First Church sanctuary at the young age of 84, nailing huge spikes into the 4' x 8' decking of laminated arches."

Fishing-Cannery Ministry

As the Chaviers ministered to their ever-growing congregation, they also continued to evangelize outside the church doors.

Desiring to reach people where they lived and worked, Dr. Chavier drove every Wednesday morning for 22 years to a "mission field" on the docks. From 1958 to 1980, he served as chaplain to one of New Bedford's largest fishing canneries, the Capeway Seafood, Inc. Donning rubber overshoes and a suit bought especially for such occasions (which were not odor-free), with Bible in hand, he made his way through the cannery's low-ceilinged, dimly lit main building, past the fish cutters whose job it was to sever heads, tails, and bones—the latter to be chopped up, minced, barreled, and sent north as bait for waiting lobstermen or as food stock for New Hampshire's mink farms. He strolled past mountains of fresh fish that made their way on conveyor belts around the processing plant. Then he hurried by the stackers, who placed the processed fish fillets into ice-cooled plastic containers, and he entered the small lounge area, where he prepared to share the gospel. The owner of the company, Al Nanfelt, had invited Dr. Chavier to speak in 15-minute combination morning-break-and-preaching services. Soon, Mr. Nanfelt extended the breaks to one half hour with pay for all who would stay and listen to Manny's Bible studies.

Some onlookers clearly showed little interest. Others, however, overtly demonstrated a hunger for the Word, hanging on every pronouncement of hope and forgiveness. A number were saved, right there on the spot.

In follow-up sessions, Pastor Chavier counseled those with problems and questions. The parsonage phone rang late into the night with calls from cannery workers whose family members were sick or dying. He was, in effect, ministering to another separate congregation. More than one of his church members came out of those makeshift chapel services in the canneries.

A Radio-Extending Ministry

Before arriving at Normandin Junior High, Pastor Chavier often started his workdays by substitute-hosting a local radio station's "Morning Meditations." Fellow faculty members at school would later stop Manny in the halls and remark, "I heard you on the air this morning." When that program's regular speaker moved to a different city to pastor, Dr. Chavier found himself standing before another open door of outreach opportunity as heir-apparent of the broadcast.

In earlier years, the armed services had sent Manny to radio school, where he'd become well versed in audio technology. He'd found the airwaves friendly to his speaking voice and style. Now, in 1964, the owners and program director of New Bedford radio station WBSM offered him a choice Sunday evening time slot for a program of his own creation and direction.

Electing to combine insights from the Word with recorded evangelistic music, Rev. Chavier introduced a 30-minute radio show, *Songs in the Night*. Listeners responded so positively that station management lengthened the program to 45 minutes, then to one full hour. The program cost First Portuguese Nazarene nothing, but Pastor Chavier was given the right to advertise services and special events. Station managers even offered the minister-broadcaster free daytime PR spots in which to plug his Sunday night hour of outreach.

The pastor soon found himself rushing from

Sunday evening services to the downtown studio to do 60 minutes of "live" radio. (This, after he had conducted two church services in the morning.)

Before long, Manuel Chavier's voice became known throughout Cape Cod. For 18 years *Songs in the Night* was aired from 10 till 11 P.M. as *the* dominant religious broadcast of the area. A consistent listening audience of over 25,000 from New Bedford to Nantucket to Martha's Vineyard sent letters and called in. Demographically, the program appealed to a wide spectrum. Roman Catholics, Jews, and Protestants came together in spirit during this hour of profound spiritual impact.

Manny featured a three-minute prayer time, introduced by the playing of chimes every week. People wrote in, asking to be remembered in prayer. There were song requests as well as a 15-minute meditation. Correspondence soared. Ratings went through the roof.

After eight years of live broadcasting, Pastor Chavier decided to tape each program, working closely with engineer Norman Aronberg. The day came when Manny led Norman and his wife, Joan, who was of Jewish descent, to the Lord. They became outstanding leaders in the church.

Ten years into his radio ministry, Dr. Chavier was presented a formal resolution by New Bedford's City Council, signed and awarded by Mayor John A. Markey. The pastor was cited for bringing "to thousands of people relief from despair and discouragement through his radio broadcast."

Songs in the Night proved to be an enormous

blessing. There were many who looked up the Chaviers' phone number in the telephone directory and called for appointments. They'd park their cars a few blocks away to protect anonymity. Manny led many program listeners to the Lord right in his own living room. They, in turn, became conduits to others who had spiritual needs.

PART THREE

*"And Will Heal
Their Land"*

6 Murder in the Streets: Turning the Ministry Tide

"Then will I hear from heaven . . . and will heal their land"
(2 Chronicles 7:14, KJV).

The Summer of Their Discontent

"It was the best of times. It was the worst of times." This famous description of life in the days of the French Revolution could have been penned to describe the events and pulse of the 1960s in America.

Since the end of World War II, the United States had known relative peace. True, the Korean War had been an unpleasant interlude. But the universally esteemed, capable general from Abilene, Kansas, had kept his word and brought American troops safely home. Prosperity had long ago replaced depression gloom and doom. GIs had returned with morale and self-confidence intact, bringing with them a sense of safety to U.S. shores and the promise of a better economy.

But the "happy days" of civil content had not

lingered. Smile-accompanied cries of "I like Ike" had given way to universal mourning over the sudden slaughter of America's bright, young president, John F. Kennedy. With the firing of a rifle from a Texas School Book Depository window, something of national innocence and youthful vigor had been taken from the American people. Trust in humankind had started to vanish, together with the golden promise of the '50s. Overseas—somewhere in the jungle-infested swampland of a place called Vietnam—sniper fire had begun to claim additional victims. Soon President Lyndon Johnson would be sending "America's best" directly into harm's way, embroiling vast numbers of troops in a no-win situation that would eventually tear the fiber of confidence in government to shreds. Watergate and the impeachment of President Richard Nixon would only add fuel to the inferno of distrust that had already been set ablaze on America's college campuses by the losses suffered in 'Nam. By the late '60s and early '70s, fewer and fewer Americans were remembering the "good times" of the '50s.

Suddenly—like hidden tectonic plates that shift without warning, causing continents to drift, collide, and erupt in almost incomprehensible earthquakes and tidal waves—unresolved racial tensions began to boil up from beneath the surface of suburban self-satisfaction, igniting heretofore-repressed tensions in many cities and towns in these seemingly United States. Few social prognosticators could have anticipated the cataclysmic upheavals that were about to shake the nation, dividing the soul of its citizenry into inequally perceived halves. Oppressed minorities were ready to let their dreams and yearnings be heard and seen as seldom before.

Cosmopolitan centers from New York to Los Angeles went up in flames, as angry young people took to the streets, hurling Molotov cocktails in an angry cry for equality and justice and setting fire to entire city centers.

New Bedford was not exempt from the rising heat of passion. The one-time whaling capital of the world was in danger of being lit with something other than spermaceti oil. With a minority population of thousands, New Bedford knew its share of the underprivileged and dissatisfied. If they had their way, this immense fishing community, nestled so peacefully beside Buzzards Bay, would lie in cinders, the smoldering residue of cultural combustion.

The month of July 1970 found New Bedford's adolescents enjoying freedom from the long New England school year. Along the docks of this bustling seaport, their fathers and brothers were unloading, sorting, and cleaning the oceanic harvests of scallops, cod, and haddock. Further inland, children had turned the narrow, snakelike streets into baseball diamonds and roller-skating rinks. Occasionally, on afternoons of sweltering heat, firefighters would turn on corner hydrants so kids could run and jump in the gushing streams. The sultry summer of the steamy south had definitely found its way north, accompanying humpback, finback, minke, right, and pilot whales on their mysterious yet predictable annual migration.

Dr. and Mrs. Chavier, needing a rest from the incessant demands of the pastorate, accepted an invitation to visit their longtime friends the Hutchinsons. The cooler climes of Bethlehem, Pennsylvania, seemed alluring, and fellowship with Neal and Edith had always been relaxing. This would be a working vacation, for Pastor Chavier would be speaking at the Bethlehem Nazarene Church the following Sunday.

What happened next is quite dramatic. "In 1965 I realized the enemy had a definite strategy, for communism was dominant in the thoughts of some people," Manny remembers. "Communists controlled half the world, and they were making inroads into the United States too. Some of their work —I discovered only as we proceeded further into the events I'm about to describe—was taking place in New Bedford!

The fires and looting, night after night, caused great concern.

"Communist sympathizers, in that period, made it a point to find every weakness in the American social structure. In the cities, they knew how to exploit those weaknesses. They fed themselves into the social fabric, wherever possible, placing themselves where they could influence moods, events, and populations. In the '60s there was a sense of loss of authority. The communists worked with an objective of destabilizing things by encouraging disrespect for teachers and government. There were flag burnings and public demonstrations. In general, the United States was experiencing social turmoil.

"The communists capitalized on all this unrest. Behind the scenes, they got quite a following and proceeded to organize their people. Their operations were well structured. In New Bedford, they took advantage of the West End, where, I later found out, their operative base was located. They set into rhythm a series of violent reactions that fed on racial and cultural considerations. They tried to make as much as possible out of existent and non-existent racial prejudices. Fires, looting, and fights were all part of their planned operation. I was somewhat innocent of their provocative methods, at the time, because our church is located in the South End. The fact is, though, they succeeded in inciting numbers of people. They set up conditions for clashes and confrontation.

"There were, in our city, certain personalities most susceptible to this sort of anger-inducement, young men who could be easily influenced by the communist agitators. In fact, some of them had played on our church's basketball team, and I had to dissolve the team because these boys were so aggressive and confrontational. Things got very hot quickly. The fires and looting, night after night, caused great concern. The mayor was not as aggressive as he might have been in dealing with the situation, but it was all new to him.

"The speaking engagement in Bethlehem, for which Betty and I had traveled so far, was scheduled July 12. My son, J. R., was watching the store, so to speak, back in New Bedford. Upon arriving in Bethlehem, I called him to find out the latest news. 'Dad, things are really getting rough!' he said. 'Last night, there were shootings and fires. So, the rebels set up barricades and blocked off the West End. You don't dare go down certain streets, or you're putting your life on the line.'

"Nine years previous to these incidents, Rose Lima, who had six children, had visited our church. She had made fun of Mary Barros, who had been converted. But when Mrs. Lima worshiped with us, the Lord dealt with her, and she was saved. Her life was dramatically changed. She left the person with whom she had been living in common law. We were able to help her straighten out some adverse circumstances, and she began to live a good life. Though her education and vocabulary were limited, she became one of our finest Sunday School teachers. She had a tremendous love for kids, and they gravitated to her like ants go after honey. With what little money she got, she bought Bibles for her students. The content of her teaching was not her strong point as much as the expressions of love that she showed her kids. They just ate it up. There was a sense of security in her presence.

"Now, almost a decade later, just an hour or so after I called J. R. from Pennsylvania, Mrs. Lima's

17-year-old son, Lester, finished a glass of milk and piece of cake in their home. As he left the house, his mother warned him, 'Don't go down to the West End.' He told her not to worry. But when he got downstairs and talked to the people around him, he said, 'I'm going where the action is.' Lester went to no-man's land. An innocent bystander, he wanted to see what was going on.

"The night before, certain young men had gone where they weren't supposed to be, and there had been shootings. Their car had been peppered with gunfire. Now, they decided to return to an area that was prepared to take them on. They made a second visit in an attempt to prove that they could drive through forbidden barriers. They came with guns blazing. Five bystanders went down, including Lester. He was killed immediately. Four others were wounded."

This terrible tragedy would be used of the Lord to put First Portuguese Church on the front page of every area newspaper and in the glare of TV lights from Providence to Boston. Rose Lima insisted to the press that her pastor would be the family's public spokesperson.

Communist agitators wanted to use Lester's murder as an excuse for whipping the city's minorities into a frenzy. The Black Panthers moved in to help foment unrest. Politicians, including U.S. Senators Edward Kennedy and Edward Brooks, called the Lima residence, offering condolences. Everyone, good and bad, wanted to involve themselves in the situation. After all, media coverage was huge.

On the day of Lester's funeral, the sidewalks and streets surrounding Colonial Funeral Parlor were thronged. At the request of the boy's mother, Dr. Chavier preached the gospel. For 55 minutes he spoke with anointing to thousands via outside loud-speakers and television cameras from five stations. Manny's remarks were based on Corinthians: "For as in Adam all die, so in Christ all will be made alive" (1 Corinthians 15:22). He contrasted the natural man with the Spirit-born. Passionately, the pastor exhorted: "This should never happen again! Christ died so that hatred need not hold sway over our lives." He tied the Lima family into the message, sharing Rose's conversion story.

That Wednesday marked an incredible turning point in the ministry of Manny Chavier.

The Lord used Manny's remarks to help diffuse the volatile social situation in the community. This was, after all, a city under siege. Nine o'clock curfews nightly had been strictly enforced in an attempt to reduce tensions. Even during the funeral, as Manny spoke, someone set off firecrackers down the street, imitating gunshots.

Pastor Chavier was uniquely inspired, on the spur of the moment, to announce a special memorial service for Lester to be held the following Sunday night at the church.

Scores of militants showed up at the cemetery committal service, raising their fists high in a demonstration of power and protest.

That Wednesday marked an incredible turning point in the ministry of Manny Chavier. The city turned to him as its voice of compassionate reason and spiritual counsel. Since Manny had known and had even pastored some of the agitators when they were children, he was one of a limited few who could go into no-man's land, walk onto the porches of would-be rioters still armed with pistols and rifles, and remain unharmed. "Don't touch Chavier!" they ordered. The young men loved and respected this servant of God.

The media gave Manny carte blanche. "Write as many newspaper articles as you wish," editors said. Radio and TV outlets craved interviews.

When Sunday came, the Lord allowed First Portuguese Church to establish itself as one of the area's most vital centers of peace. Rose Lima, who had buried her son four days earlier, asked Dr. Chavier for the privilege of giving her testimony in Lester's memorial service. The church was packed with civic dignitaries as well as representatives from the religious world. Supernaturally strengthened by the Holy Spirit, the grieving mother stood, serenely composed, before the assembly. "I feel sorry for the boys who killed my son," she declared. She then tied her ability to forgive to the wondrous work of grace that had taken place in her life nine years previously. Her words left the audience in tears. Afterward, many exclaimed, "Isn't it wonderful when Christianity is real!"

In the ensuing months, Manuel Chavier continued to have open access to the media, as he represented the family in its response to all pretrial and trial developments. This meant ongoing, front-page newspaper publicity for the church.

The community got behind the financial responsibilities of the tragedy. They wanted to pay for the casket, the funeral, the gravesite, the stone—everything. They channeled all the money through First Portuguese Church, giving Manny's congregation still more visibility.

On May 18, 1971, when the amazing and unexpected verdict of "not guilty" was delivered by a jury, Dr. Chavier shared with the public Rose's decision not to appeal. "Enough blood has been shed," she told lawyers who were eager to pursue the case on a pro bono basis. By remaining a steadfast witness for Christ, Rose allowed the Lord to start healing the city's wounds.

From Riots to Revival: Going International

"By your blood you ransomed for God saints from every tribe and language and people and nation" (Revelation 5:9, NRSV).

A Table-Turning Event

What happened next is marvelous. Scores of newcomers, all non-Cape Verdeans, started visiting Manny's church: Yankees, African-Americans, French, Italians, Latin Americans, Norwegians, Poles, and Germans. A steady stream of people poured in from differing classes of society.

At first, Dr. Chavier felt they should go elsewhere; for, in his mind, their presence didn't conform to the Portuguese culture. He had seen himself as "missionary" to his own people. "You're in the wrong place. You need to try First Church," he told the visitors.

Soon God spoke to Manny, saying, "I didn't send these crowds to First Church!" Distinctly, the Lord insisted, "I sent them to *your* congregation!"

"I felt guilty, then, of prejudice-in-reverse," Dr. Chavier says. "I was neutralizing the work of the

Holy Spirit. With the Lord's intervention, a riot turned into revival! We changed our attitude and began welcoming our non-Cape Verdean friends. God called me to minister to them, too, and I watched what happened to our church."

For several years, 80-plus percent of the Portuguese Nazarene membership had been Cape Verdean. Suddenly 50 percent of worshipers were from other cultures.

The tide had turned!

Extended-Service Opportunities

The city opened its arms to Pastor Chavier in ever-widening opportunities for service. New Bedford's business leaders had taken note of Manny's judgment, abilities, and selflessness. Before long, his time and wisdom were much in demand. The inner halls of commerce and industry became his pulpit; the city's leaders, another congregation.

In the years that followed, this Nazarene pastor served his city as president of the Kiwanis Club; trustee and chair of the New Bedford Free Public Library; director of the Boys' Club; president of the Legal Aid Services Society with daily access to area courtrooms and judges; member of the local American Red Cross; advisory board member of The Salvation Army; director of the Concentrated Employment Program; vice chairman of the Commonwealth Electric Advisory Board; director of the Fall River Christian Day School; trustee of New Bedford Institution for Savings (which, ironically, had once turned down his loan application); and member of the Mayor's Focus Committee.

Name-Change Necessity

With its explosive growth in social diversity, community influence, and church attendance, the First Portuguese Church of the Nazarene was compelled to reassess its name and image. In 1978, the church board voted to charter the fellowship as International Church of the Nazarene, reflecting its multicultural constituency.

Just as the old name seemed an inadequate description of the expanding church body, the Purchase Street facility also failed to house International Church's widening outreach ministries.

With $60,000 of donated architectural plans, Manny undertook the building of a new, 500-seat sanctuary in back of the old church. The generous architect's gift came from Robert R. Gurney, a 37-year-old Episcopalian New England Telephone construction manager with a degree in structural civil engineering, who had been deeply touched by a message Dr. Chavier had preached.

Vinal Savage, a 67-year-old mason who had heard Dr. Chavier speak in Dennisport, Massachusetts, put up most of the edifice's 64,000 bricks. Mr. Savage traveled 12,000 miles during one year to do so. And he wouldn't accept a dime!

The new Pleasant Street sanctuary, which cost half the original estimate, was dedicated on November 11, 1984.

Groundbreaking for new sanctuary in 1983

International Church of the Nazarene today

I had the thrill of participating in that service, attended by a record crowd of 800. J. R. Chavier and the choir presented our musical Peace in the Storm *in the afternoon.*

8 "It's the Lord!": Celebrating a Life of Service

"For the Lord God . . . bestows favor and honor. No good thing does the Lord withhold from those who walk uprightly" (Psalm 84:11, NRSV).

His manner evangelically unoffensive, yet unapologetically pastoral, Manuel Chavier has been at ease with doctors, judges, bankers, lawyers, school superintendents, and CEOs.

With a half century of service to his community behind him, this dedicated servant of God has also been a faithful and trusted adviser to his denomination and other Christian organizations. Dr. Chavier was a trustee of Eastern Nazarene College for several years. He has been a valued member of the New England District Advisory Board, Sunday School Ministries Board, Ministerial Credentials Committee, Court of Appeals, Christian Action Committee, and Board of Evangelism. Perhaps most notably, he served on the General Board of the International Church of the Nazarene for 6 years (1990-96) and Committee for Minority Groups in the United States. He has been president of the

Cape Verdean Bible Conference for 23 years, a non-Nazarene group that provides counsel, services, and support for newcomers to the United States. And he is president of Smith Mills Camp Meeting Association in Dartmouth, Massachusetts.

Pastor Chavier has lived to see International Church minister weekly to 400 people of diverse cultural backgrounds. Through them his professional and worldwide influence has touched thousands more. For his work in New Bedford, the city honored him with the coveted Duncan A. Dottin Human Relations Award.

With church properties valued in excess of $2.5 million, Pastor Chavier finds his greatest joy in watching church-related programs touch lives for Christ. A Friday Night Bible School ministers to a hundred or so unchurched children from nearby housing projects. In addition, the church sponsors Women of the Word (WOW); Men of the Word (MOW); Operation Care (designed to feed the hungry, help unwed mothers, and take comfort to the sick and afflicted); and J. R. Chavier's classes for the divorced and addicted.

Manny Chavier is still a soul winner. Wherever he goes, he leaves reminders of divine will and purpose behind. He prays with all he meets, unabashedly asking for the privilege. His motives are unquestioned by those who know him; his intercessions, gratefully welcomed.

Manuel and Betty Chavier would be the last persons to take credit for the miracles they have seen in New Bedford. "It's the Lord! It's the Lord!"

Manny repeats over and over. "We watched God do it all. We couldn't do any of it. Betty and I are just His servants. God accomplished the task to which He called us. No matter where I go in this whole story, it's the Lord!"

The people who have seen the International Church story unfold, however, recognize in the Chaviers "saints in the making." Therefore, it should not be a surprise that New Bedford's brightest and best chose to honor Dr. Chavier in 1997 with a permanent tribute. Hiring professional artist Deborah Beth Macy, city fathers commissioned a full-length oil portrait of this Nazarene pastor to be painted and framed. Then, invitations went out to several area representatives for an official unveiling of the completed work. A much publicized evening of honors, speeches, and a reception followed, during which city council members, business representatives, educators, and the mayor took turns, expressing gratitude on behalf of the citizenry of New Bedford for Manuel Chavier's selfless ministry and contributions to the community.

Manuel Chavier's service to Christ has been on behalf of his community. He has connected deeply to people's lives. Hundreds, if not thousands, of interconnections have resulted in a vast network of affiliations and associations. Manny has touched the command and control centers of commerce, education, and civic life in greater New Bedford with the gospel. "The fisherman's pastor" has become a valued friend and respected adviser of mayors, school committee personnel, and jurists.